LEARN TO DRAW

DISNEY · PIXAR

BRAVE

Learn to draw Merida,
Elinor, Angus, and other characters
from Disney/Pixar's *Brave*
step by step!

Illustrated by The Disney Storybook Artists

Walter Foster

7 9 10 8 6

TABLE OF CONTENTS

❋ THE STORY OF BRAVE ❋

Merida is the adventurous Princess of DunBroch, who is more comfortable shooting her bow than wearing ball gowns. Independent and feisty, Merida is horrified that her parents have invited the lords of three neighboring clans to bring their sons to the castle for a competition—where the prize is Merida's hand in marriage!

Determined to avoid the fate that awaits her, Merida defies this age-old tradition and instead participates in the archery competition to win her own hand in marriage. She shoots all three bullseyes to win the competition, but her defiance causes a ruckus in the kingdom and an argument with her mother. Merida runs away and rides into the forest on her horse, Angus. She soon comes across a witch who gives her a spell cake that, Merida hopes, will change her mother's mind about the princess's marriage.

As soon as Elinor eats the cake, she is transformed into a bear. As Merida and Elinor fight to transform Elinor back into the queen she is, they embark on a journey of bravery to prove that love can beat all odds.

TOOLS AND MATERIALS

Before you begin, gather some drawing tools, such as paper,
a regular pencil, an eraser, and a pencil sharpener. For color, you can use
markers, colored pencils, crayons, or even paint!

drawing pencil
and paper

eraser

sharpener

colored
pencils

felt-tip
markers

paintbrush
and paints

HOW TO USE THIS BOOK

Follow the steps like the ones shown below, and you will be
drawing Merida, the triplet cubs, and the other characters
from *Brave* in no time!

First draw basic shapes
using light lines that will
be easy to erase.

Each new step is shown in
blue, so you'll know what to
add next.

Follow the blue lines to
draw the details.

Now darken the lines you want
to keep, and erase the rest.

Use some magic (or crayons
or markers) to add color to
your drawing!

DRAWING EXERCISES

Warm up your hand by drawing squiggles and shapes on a piece of scrap paper.

Draw a square

Draw a circle

Draw an oval

Draw a rectangle

Draw a triangle

If you can draw a few basic shapes, you can draw just about anything!

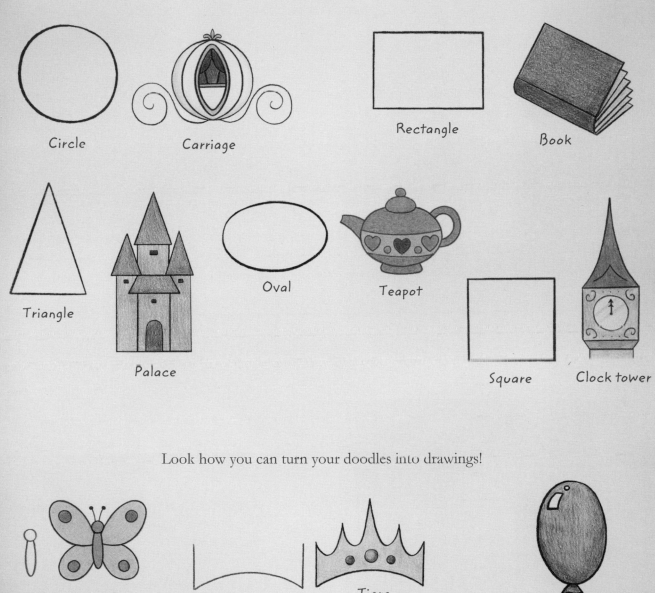

Circle

Carriage

Rectangle

Book

Triangle

Palace

Oval

Teapot

Square

Clock tower

Look how you can turn your doodles into drawings!

Butterfly

Tiara

Balloon

Gown

Bird

MERIDA

Merida is the adventurous Princess of DunBroch. More comfortable in the woods with her bow than in a ball gown, Merida would be perfectly content to ride her horse, Angus, around all day in the sunshine.

for Merida's hair, use wild, squiggly lines

Merida's eyes

NO!   YES!

MERIDA IN ACTION

Fergus and Elinor invited the lords of the Highland clans to present their sons as suitors in a competition to win Merida's hand in marriage. To avoid marrying one of the lords' sons, Merida shocks everyone by competing for her own hand in the archery competition. She hits each bullseye to win the competition, but in the process she causes a ruckus in the kingdom.

profile is cur[...]

small nose

ANGUS

Angus is Merida's trusty Clydesdale horse. Though he doesn't talk, he seems to understand Merida better than anyone else, and he plays with her and comforts her whenever she needs it.

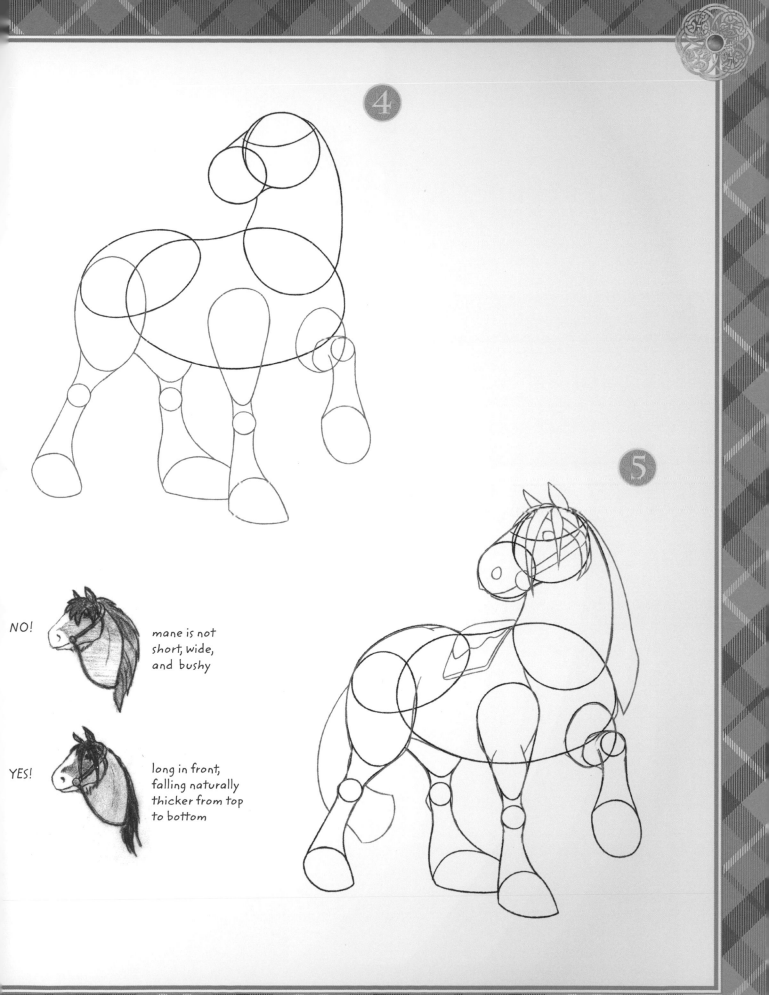

4

5

NO!

mane is not
short, wide,
and bushy

YES!

long in front,
falling naturally
thicker from top
to bottom

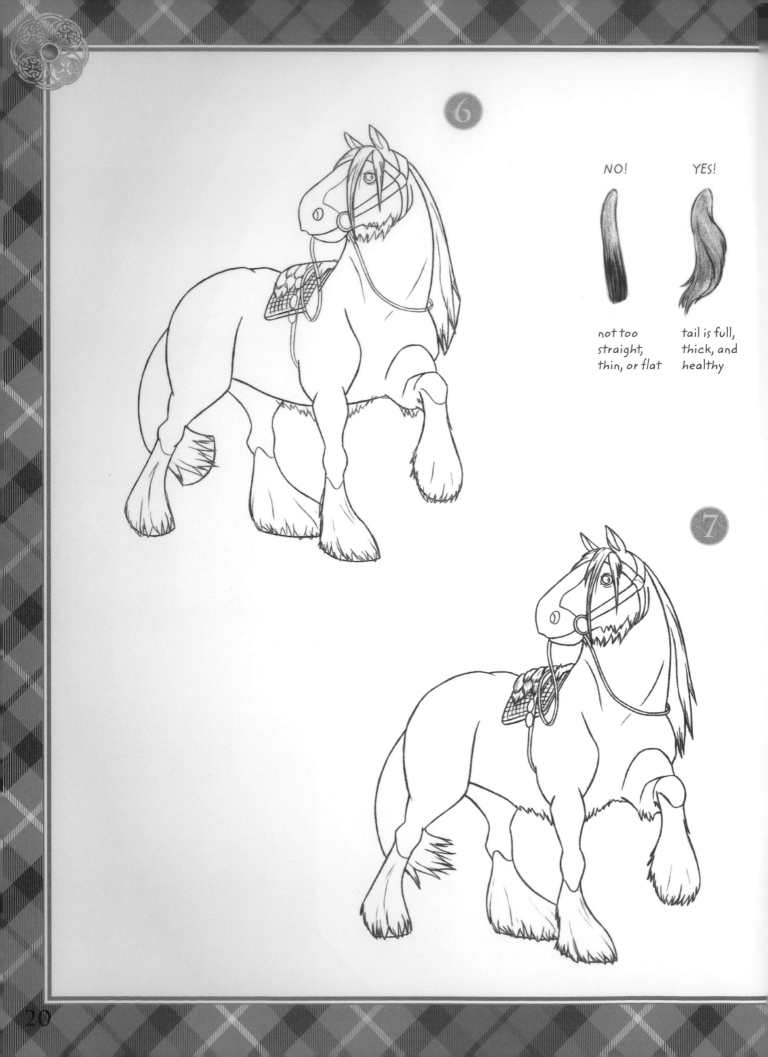

6

NO!

YES!

not too
straight,
thin, or flat

tail is full,
thick, and
healthy

7

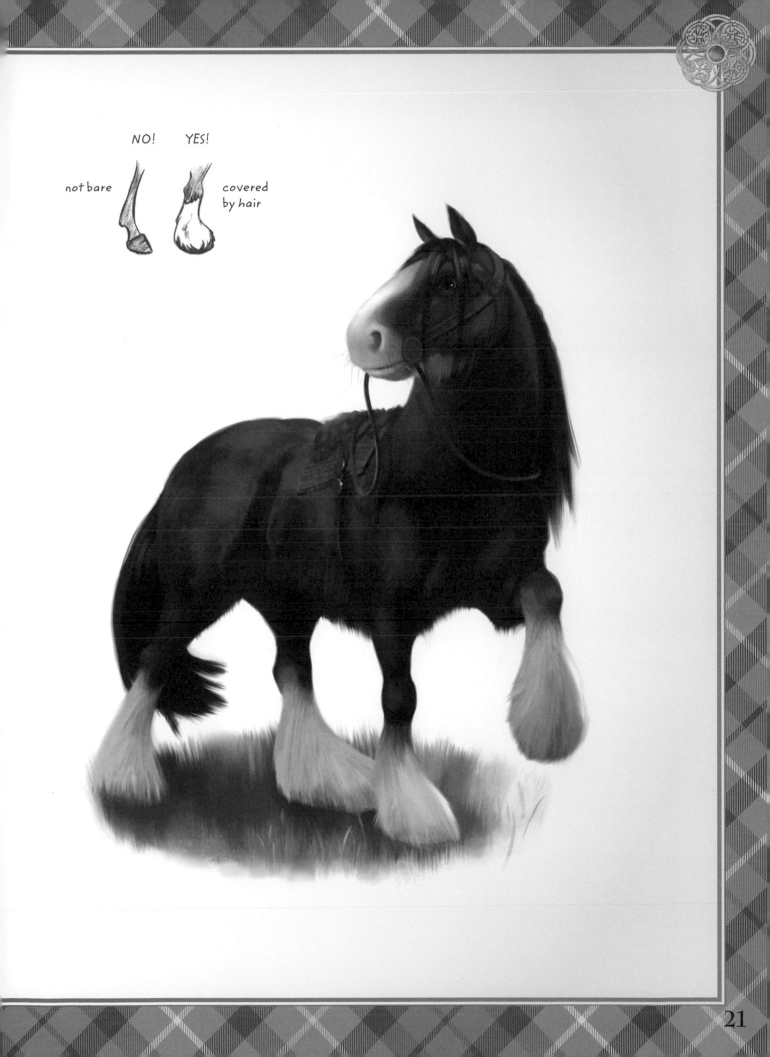

NO!   YES!

not bare   covered by hair

QUEEN ELINOR

As Queen of DunBroch, Elinor relies on tradition and diplomacy to rule the kingdom. Though she carries a lot of responsibility, there is a strong spirit inside Elinor that allows her to eventually connect with her audacious daughter, Merida.

④

NO!   no individual
lashes

YES!   eye is almond
shaped, with one
line for eyelashes

⑤

6

7

profile is straight
and angular

straight-on view

NO!   YES!

no straight
lines—hair
looks too flat

ribbon should
be curved, not
straight, to give
weight and
dimension to hair

side view
close up

hair is straight
and heavy in a
long ponytail

KING FERGUS

An adventurer at heart, Fergus is always eager to teach his daughter, Merida, a thing or two on the bow and sword. Years ago, to save Elinor and Merida, Fergus fought the vicious bear Mor'du and lost his leg, but that hasn't dampened his jovial nature.

NO!

YES!

not too
many studs

helmet
is small

NO!

YES!

not too
skinny

lines of
woodgrain
not too straight

leg is wider
at the top

woodgrain has
lots of swirly
knots & burls

6

7

ELINOR THE BEAR

Elinor is transformed into a bear when she eats a cake that the Witch gave to Merida.
Merida and Elinor the Bear embark on a journey to find the Witch to change Elinor back,
and in the process, mother and daughter grow closer than ever.

NO!   not spaced
       too evenly

YES!   five claws
       grouped
       together

6

NO!   YES!

not   ears
pointy   rounded

no cartoony eyes

7

ELINOR THE BEAR IN ACTION

Elinor the Bear isn't sure what to eat one morning, so Merida teaches her how to fish like a real bear.
Reluctant at first, Elinor the Bear finally joins in and plays in the stream with Merida.

④

NO!   YES!

not too fuzzy   fur is smooth

⑤

NO!   YES!

not too big   nose & eyes
and round   proportioned

MOR'DU IN ACTION

Mor'du is the monstrous bear that interrupted a royal family picnic when Merida was just a wee lass. Years later, Merida and Elinor discover that Mor'du is actually a cursed ancient prince.

4

five claws

NO! YES!

nose

NO! YES!

ear

5

bald patches
and many scars

left eye
is blind
(white) an
has a scar

scars on
Mor'du's
nose

THE WITCH

Because she is a reluctant witch, the Witch disguises herself as a wood-carver.
In Merida's desperate attempt to fix things with her mother, Merida finally convinces
the reluctant Witch to make a spell cake to give her mother, in hopes that it will make
Elinor change her mind about Merida's betrothal.

thin gnarled
fingers with
large knuckles

wears ring with
symbol of two
crossed axes

necklace and
bangles made
from shells,
bones, and rock

hair lays back

one eye open,
one eye shut

left ear has
one large
earring

YES!

whiskers
on chin

large
nose

NO!

hair does
not sit up on
top of head

companion is a
black raven

YES!   NO!

right ear   not small
is large with   or pointy
earrings

THE TRIPLETS

Harris, Hubert, and Hamish are Merida's identical-triplet brothers. Though they are troublemakers, they adore Merida and would do anything for her.

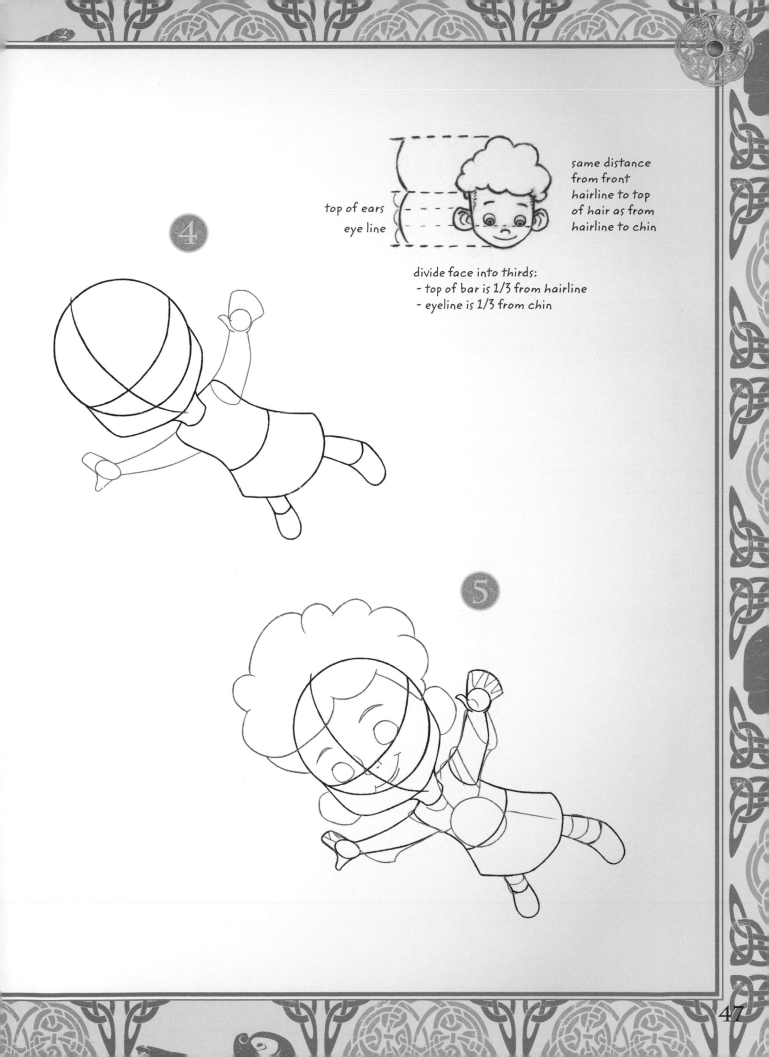

same distance
from front
hairline to top
of hair as from
hairline to chin

top of ears

eye line

divide face into thirds:
- top of bar is 1/3 from hairline
- eyeline is 1/3 from chin

a few
loose hairs

6

curly hair
on top,
cut short
on the
sides

NO!

pupils and
eyes not
too large

7

THE TRIPLET CUBS

Harris, Hubert, and Hamish eat some of the cake that Merida brought back from the Witch, so they all turn into bears just like their mother. Even though they're bear cubs, they still know when Merida's in trouble, and they love to come to her rescue.

eyes sit about 1/4
of the way from
bottom of head

top of nose
sits on bottom
of eyeline

④

NO!

eyes cannot
move like this

YES!

eyes set close
together

⑤

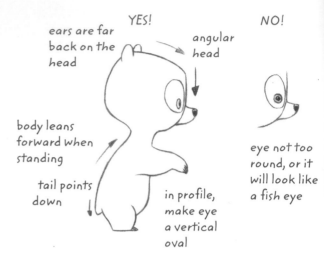

YES!

ears are far back on the head

angular head

NO!

body leans forward when standing

tail points down

in profile, make eye a vertical oval

eye not too round, or it will look like a fish eye

6

YES! ear like this

NO! ear does not lay down

NO! not fuzzy and round

7

THE SONS OF LORDS MACGUFFIN, MACINTOSH, AND DINGWALL

Lords MacGuffin, MacIntosh, and Dingwall are the three lords of the Highland kingdom, and they haven't always gotten along. Even in this time of peace, they don't hesitate to let their sons—Young MacGuffin, Young MacIntosh, and Wee Dingwall—compete against each other for Merida's hand in marriage.

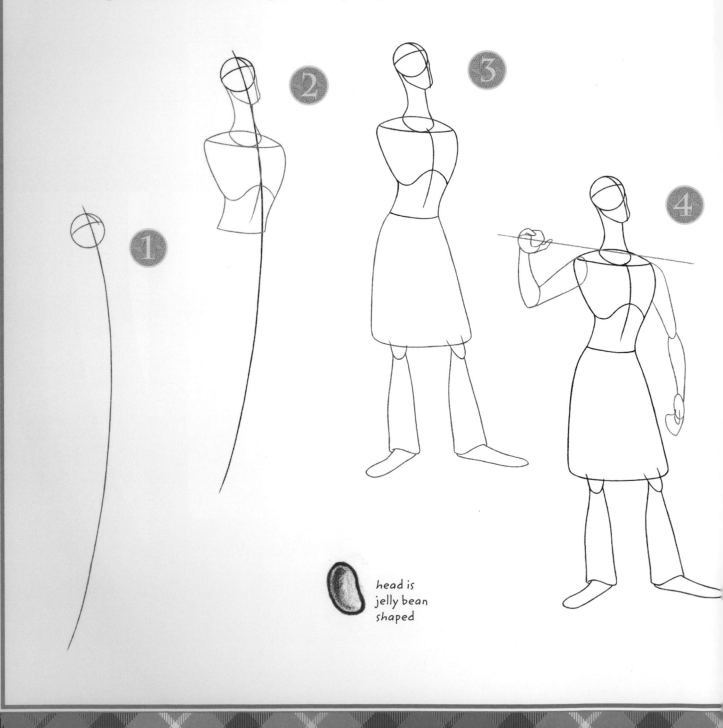

head is jelly bean shaped

⑤ ⑥ ⑦

*Young
MacIntosh*

*Lord
MacIntosh*

NO!

hair not
too big and
poofy

YES!

hair is
wavy, curly,
and large

body comparison

① ② ③ ④

Dingwall's hair stands straight up

not too stiff

head is football shaped

5

6

7

Wee
Dingwall

Lord
Dingwall

YES! braids follow shape of head

head is pear shaped

NO! not too poofy or round

5

6

7

Young
MacGuffin

Lord
MacGuffin

THE CASTLE

The castle in the Scottish Highlands is home to Fergus; Elinor; Merida; and the triplets, Harris, Hubert, and Hamish. The Highland games take place here, where Merida shocks the whole kingdom.

THE END

Now that you've learned the secrets to drawing the characters from *Brave*, try creating scenes from the movie or original scenes of your very own. You can draw Merida shooting her bow in a field or riding her horse through the forest, the triplets running through the hallways or causing mischief in the kingdom, or Fergus and Elinor laughing together. With the skills you've learned, the possibilities are endless! To be the maker of your own story, just like Merida, all you need is a piece of paper, a pencil, and your imagination!